Find Draw It Books on social media:

@drawitbooks
#drawitbooks #drawityourself
#drawnfrommemory

Paperback ISBN: 979-8-840-39208-9

www.draw-it-books.com

Cover Design:
Lorraine Inglis
www.lorraineinglisdesign.co.uk

Spanish Drawn from Memory
101 words and phrases

Contents **Contenido**

Discover more at

www.draw-it-books.com

Follow

@drawitbooks

to stay up to date on all things **Draw It Books!**

Why this book works
Por qué este libro funciona

Why this book works

These are the reasons why this book works:

It's fun
Learning is simply better when it's fun.

Mnemonics
Mnemonics is the study of memory. Draw It Books uses mnemonics to help the information really stick in your mind.

Logical and illogical
Draw It Books helps bring together a healthy balance of logical and illogical thinking.

Active engagement
Draw It Books encourages a more active, not passive, approach to learning, where you, the reader, engage and participate more in the learning process. Because you take more ownership of the learning process information will stick better in your mind.

How this book works
Cómo funciona este libro

How this book works

The Drawn from Memory language series uses a range of concepts and techniques to help you build your language vocabulary in a fun, efficient, and effective way.

Some of the main concepts and techniques used include:

- Mnemonics and associations
- Acceptance that language changes
- Descriptivism, prescriptivism, and ambiscriptivism
- Linguistics
- Syncretism and synthesis
- The 6 C's: Composure, clarity, confidence, creativity, commitment, and courage
- You have the tools to go at your own pace
- Growth mindset
- Visualisation

In this section a brief explanation of the concepts and techniques used in this book is explained. If you wish to, please research these topics in more detail to support your learning journey.

Mnemonics and associations

Mnemonics is the study of memory. As this book is about building your vocabulary, you need a way to store information efficiently in your mind. Mnemonics helps us to do this by creatively using associations to store information. Associations are often picture, sound, word, or movement based.

Acceptance that language changes

Language has changed and evolved a lot over time. It will continue to do so. Remember, the dictionary does not contain 'real words' it contains the words that society recognises and most commonly uses. Language is an ever-changing thing. Strive to change appropriately with it. This means that the rules you know now may have to adapt and evolve as language adapts and evolves. If you need to use slang, then use slang.

Prescriptivism, Descriptivism, and Ambiscriptivism

These topics can help us balance our understanding of language, how it changes, and how we can change with it. Prescriptivism is a strict approach to language that says, 'this is how it must be used'. Descriptivism is a more creative approach towards language that says, 'this is how language is actually used'. Ambiscriptivism is a term that we can use to help us blend these two schools of thought. It allows us to have a standard that gives us a consistency and foundation to learning language (prescriptivism). It also gives us the opportunity to apply creativity and flexibility so that we can adapt and evolve with language (descriptivism).

Linguistics

Linguistics is the study of language. It is made up of many topics that explore the use of things like words, symbols, patterns, sounds, sentences, and more. Developing your understanding of linguistics is key to learning language.

Syncretism and synthesis

Syncretism and synthesis are two words that help us to explain what it is we are trying to achieve. They are both ways of explaining 'connecting things together'. What we are trying to do is join what we already know with more information. This is why mnemonics is so useful; because it helps us do that in an efficient, but fun and enjoyable way.

The 6 C's: Composure, clarity, confidence, creativity, commitment, and courage

These are some key qualities that we want to acknowledge and embrace when we are trying to learn. If at any point learning becomes boring or a struggle, remember that it is normal to find learning difficult at times. Just remember if we apply these qualities to our attitude and mentality towards learning we will find a way to overcome any challenges we face and make progress.

You have the tools to go at your own pace

This book is a great tool that you can use to help you learn. But self-motivation is the key to any successful learning. Find your style and go at the pace you want to go at.

Growth mindset

It is vital that we adopt a growth mindset throughout our learning journey. This attitude will help us to remember that 'every day is a learning day' and that learning and growth are positive things that we can use and experience to achieve more.

A growth mindset helps us to develop our Comfort Zone, embrace change, respond positively to Fight or Flight situations, and develop resilience.

Visualisation

Visualisation is the overall goal here. Being able to access and engage our mind's eye.

This ability to access your imagination and be creative is a fantastic transferable skill that you can apply to all areas of learning.

Drawing is encouraged in this book because it helps to stimulate and develop our ability to visualise. But if you feel you already have the ability to visualise, or don't feel like drawing, then you can write or just use your imagination and ability to visualise.

How to use this book
Cómo usar este libro

How to use this book

Each page provides you with this format:

English Word
Spanish Word (gender)
(Phonetics)
Imagery suggestion

English word – This will likely be a word you have heard of before.

Spanish word – This is a translation of the English word into Spanish. If present, the letter in brackets indicate the gender of the word; masculine or feminine.

Phonetics – This is how to pronounce the Spanish word using some sounds from English.

Imagery suggestion – This is a suggestion of an image you can use to help remember the Spanish word. If you want to come up with your own imagery, do it. Your imagination will sometimes do this for you anyway. Make things as simple or complex as you want.

An important thing to remember is that, to begin with, the parts of this learning process may not make sense. But give it a chance and experiment with being creative. The images that you create are there to help you link the words and information from one language to another. Remember links are often picture, sound, word, or movement based.

The imagery suggestions won't always be 'perfect' matches. But the imagery suggestions will give you enough information to create a link between languages. Treat these links like prompts that you can use to help you recall information.

Sometimes the links are very logical; because the Spanish and English are so similar. When this happens use an iconic thing from the language to link to, like the Spanish flag.

Please note: This book is a very basic standard. Whilst there is detail about word gender this is a not the focus of this book. This information can be learned later. For now, enjoy building your vocabulary with this basic method.

The Alphabet
El Alfabeto / El Abecedario

The Alphabet

A really important part of learning a language is understanding it's alphabet. Spanish has a very accessible alphabet.

When you are trying to read a word in Spanish, the majority of the time you can simply pronounce, or sound out, the letters from the alphabet and that is how the word will sound when you say it.

Naturally, there are some exceptions. But this book explains how to pronounce each word phonetically in every example.

For example:

Spanish for 'no problem' is 'de nada'.
You can say 'de nada' broken down like this:
duh-eh nuh-ah-duh-ah

then more joined up like this:
deh nah-dah

de nada

The Alphabet
El Alfabeto or El Abecedario

Below is a list explaining how you pronounce letters in Spanish when you use them to say words. Think of them like little jigsaw pieces that you stick together to make a word.

Letter sounds – Used when saying words

Letter	Pronunciation	Letter	Pronunciation
a	ah	n	nuh
b	buh	ñ	nyuh
c	kah / ss	o	oh
ch	ch	p	puh
d	duh	q	kuh
e	eh	r	ruh
f	fuh	rr	rrr
g	guh / huh	s	suh
h	*silent*	T	tuh
i	ee	U	uh
j	huh	V	vuh
k	kuh	W	wuh
l	luh	X	kuss / zyuh
ll	yuh	y	yuh / ee
m	muh	Z	thuh / suh

The Alphabet
El Alfabeto or El Abecedario

Below is how you pronounce the names of the letters in Spanish. You can use this when you are explaining how to spell words.

Letter names – Used when spelling out words

Letter	Pronunciation	Letter	Pronunciation
a	ah	n	en-eh
b	beh	ñ	en-yeh
c	seh	o	oh
ch	cheh	p	peh
d	deh	q	koo
e	eh	r	er-eh
f	ef-eh	rr	erreh
g	heh / guh	s	ess-eh
h	ach-eh	T	teh
i	ee	U	oo
j	ho-tah	V	veh
k	kah	W	dob-leh-veh
l	el-eh	X	eh-kees
ll	eh-yeh	y	ee-gri-eh-gah
m	em-eh	Z	seh-tah

Example
Ejemplo

Example

thank you
gracias
(grah-see-ass)
An ass with grass growing on its ass, saying "thank you" to someone.
(Like on the cover).

Read the English word.
Read the Spanish word.
Read the phonetic breakdown of how to pronounce the word.
Read the imagery suggestion.

Then...

you can use the space below to draw your version of this image

or...

come up with your own image and create that.

You can draw, you can cut out pictures and stick them in, or you can just write a description of an image that helps you remember the word.
Whatever works for you.

General Conversations
Conversacion General

hello
hola
(oh-la)

Someone using a *hula* hoop and holding another *hula* hoop (a giant O) in their hand and using it to wave *hello*.

my name is...

mi nombre es...

(me nom-breh ess...)
Someone 'nomming' on bread
while trying to say, "my name is...".

goodbye
adíos
(ah-dee-oss)
Someone *adding ears* to the side of a sign made of giant letters that spells 'goodbye'.

yes

sí

(see)

A giant *yes* floating in the *sea*.

no

no

(noh)

A Spanish flag with 'no' written on it.

please

por favor

(por fah-vor)

A *poor* person asking for a *favour*.

thank you

gracias

(grah-see-ass)

An ass with *grass* growing on its *ass* saying, "thank you" to someone. A 'grassy ass'.

sorry

perdón

(pehr-don)

A giant *pear* bumping into people saying, "sorry".

excuse me

disculpa

(diss-kul-pah)

Someone getting someone's attention(excuse me) by tapping on their shoulder with a *disc.*
(think CD/Floppy Disc).

no problem

de nada

(deh nah-dah)

An *adder* living in a *den* with
no problems and no worries. A 'den adder'.

I don't understand

no entiendo

(no en-tee-en-doh)

A *no entry sign* on your forehead; because information isn't going in and you *don't understand*.

I would like...

quisiera...

(key-see-air-ah)

I would like to see a *key* flying out of the *sea* into the *air* (like a dolphin jumping into the air).

help

ayudar

(ah-yoo-dar)

Someone asking for *help* by saying, "are you there".

Questions
Preguntas

how do you say?

¿cómo se dice...?

(koh-moh seh dee-seh)
A *comma* rolling *dice* with 'how do you say?' written on the side of them.

what...?

¿qué...?

(keh)

A 'mystery *kettle*' with a question mark on the side of it making you wonder *what*'s inside.

where...?

¿dónde...?

(don-deh)

The *Don* from the mob
asking, *"where* is my daughter?"

how…?

¿cómo…?

(koh-moh)

You see a *comma* with a moustache(*mo*) and wonder *how* a *comma* got a moustache.

when...?

¿cuando...?

(kwan-doh)

A person waiting outside tae*kwon*do class
wondering '*when* does it start?'

why...?

¿por qué...?

(por keh)

A piece of *pork* sat wondering
'*why* am I a piece of *pork*?'

who?

¿quién...?

(key-ehn)

A *key* with a *hen*'s body(key hen) pretending
to be an owl saying, "hoo hoo".
(*who? who?*)

which...?

¿cuál...?

(kwal)

A job interviewer asking,
"which qualifications do you have?"

what time?

¿qué hora...?

(keh or-ah)

A letter *K* with an *aura* around it wondering 'what time...?'.

how much?

¿cuanto...?

(kwan-toh)

A game at a fairground where you guess how much a *quantity* of *toes* weighs.

(Imagine all the toes in a jar at a fairground).

do you have?

¿tienes...?

(tee-ehn-ess)

Someone asking a shop keeper, "do you have a cup of *tea* with an *N* and *S* floating in it?"

Things
Cosas

food

alimento (m.)

(al-ee-men-toh)

A group of men (*all the men*) putting food into a *toe*.

drink
bebida (f.)
(beh-bee-dah)
A *baby* having a *drink* with their *dada*.

pen

lápiz (m.)

(lah-peeth)

Someone who has *pens* for *teeth* and the pieces of *pen* have fallen on to their *lap*.

paper

papel (m.)

(pah-pel)

A *propellor* made out of *paper*.

Times of day
Momentos del Día

day
día (m.)
(dee-ah)
A *deer* walking around enjoying the *day*.

now
ahora
(ah-or-ah)

An aura around you in this moment right *now*.

today

hoy

(oy)

Today on a calendar shouting, "oi".

yesterday

ayer
(ah-yer)

Someone remembering what happened *yesterday* and saying, "ah yeah".

tomorrow / morning

mañana

(man-nyan-ah)
A man made out of a *banana*
going to bed ready for *tomorrow*. /
A man made out of a *banana*
getting up out of bed in the *morning*.

midday / noon

mediodía (m.)

(med-ee-oh-dee-ah)

A *medic* having a standoff(cowboy style) with a *deer* at midday(*noon*).

afternoon

tarde (f.)

(tar-deh)

A giant jam *tart* playing in the *afternoon*.

evening / night

noche (f.)

(noh-cheh)

The moon in the *night* sky with a *notch* in it.

breakfast

desayuno (m.)

(deh-say-oo-noh)

Someone who is *dizzy* trying to eat their *breakfast* and saying, "oo no".

lunch
almuerzo (m.)
(al-moo-air-thoh)

An *almond*, that is *mooing*, having lunch floating in the *air*.

dinner

cena (f.)

(sen-ah)

A *sinner* praying for *dinner*.

Pronouns
Pronombres

I

yo
(yoh)
You on your own, playing with a big *yo-yo* that looks
like an *eye*.

me

mí

(mee)

A Spanish flag with 'me' written on it.

we

nosotros (m.) / nosotras (f.)

(noh-soh-tross / noh-soh-trass)

A group(we) of flying *noses* with wings like *albatross* / tails like *asses*.

you

tú

(too)

You, pointing at another person wearing a *tutu*.

they, them
ellos (m.) / ellas (f.)
(eh-yoss / eh-yass)
You, pointing at a group(them) of E's with *ears* /
riding *asses*.

Buildings
Edificios

hotel

hotel (m.)

(oh-tel)

A Spanish flag with 'hotel' written on it.

airport

aeropuerto (m.)

(air-oh-poo-air-toh)

An *airport* made of *poo* with flying '*toe*-planes' in it.

station
estación (f.)
(ess-tah-see-on)
A train *station* made out of
the letter *S* with a *C on* top.

port

puerto (m.)

(poo-air-toh)

A port with boats that are made of *poo* and *hairy toes*.

petrol station

gasolinera (f.)

(gah-soh-leen-air-ah)

A *gas* can dancing around a petrol station like a *ballerina*.

pharmacy

farmacia (f.)

(farm-ah-see-ah)

A Spanish flag with 'pharmacy' written on it.

hospital

hospital (m.)
(oh-spit-al)
A Spanish flag with 'hospital' written on it.

bank

banco (m.)

(ban-koh)

A Spanish flag with 'bank' written on it.

shop

tienda (f.)

(tee-en-dah)

A row of shops with a building shaped like a big letter *T* at the start and a building shaped like a big letter *A* on the *end*.

restaurant

restaurante (m.)

(rest-ow-ran-teh)

A Spanish flag with 'restaurant' written on it.

cafe

café (m.)

(kah-feh)

A Spanish flag with 'café' written on it.

supermarket

supermercado (m.)

(soo-peh-meh-kah-doh)

A car with a cape on (*supercar*) going around the *supermarket* buying an *avocado*.

Landmarks
Puntos de referencia

road
calle (f.)
(kah-yeh)
Someone rowing a *kayak* down the
middle of the *road*.

beach

playa (f.)

(plah-ya)

A pair of *pliers* sunbathing on the *beach*.

sea

mar (m./f.)

(mar)

A *grandma* floating in the *sea*.

Rooms / Furniture
Habitaciones / Muebles

toilets

aseos (m.)

(ass-eh-os)

Someone wiping their *ass* after going to the *toilet*.

floor

piso (m.)

(pee-soh)

Someone *peeing* on the *floor*.

stairs

escalera (f.)

(ess-kah-leh-rah)

Someone *escaping* a fire by *scaling* a flight of *stairs*.

lift

ascensor (m.)

(ass-sen-sor)

Someone *ascending* off the ground in a *lift*.

Transport

Transporte

taxi

taxi (m.)

(tak-see)

A Spanish flag with 'taxi' written on it.

bus

autobús (m.)

(ow-toh-boos)

Someone getting *out of a bus*.

car
coche (m.)
(koh-cheh)
Someone 'cotching' in their car.

train

tren (m.)

(tr-ehn)

A *trendy train* wearing sunglasses.

airplane

avión (m.)

(ah-vee-on)

A plane with 'V-shaped' wings on it.

boat / ferry

barco (m.)

(bar-koh)

A *barking boat* about to *embark* on a journey.

Directions
Direcciones

here

aquí

(ah-key)

A map with a door *key* on it showing 'you are here'.

forwards

adelante

(ad-el-an-teh)

Advancing forwards across the Atlantic.

backwards

atrás

(ah-tr-ass)

Someone flicking through an *atlas backwards*.

left
izquierdo (m.) / izquierda (f.)
(is-key-air-dah/doh)
There are two mystery boxes next to each other. A caveman is pointing at the box on the left with their left hand and asking, "is key there?"

right
derecho (m.) / derecha (f.)
(deh-reh-cho/cha)
A letter D is *retching* and trying to cover its mouth with its right hand.

up / above

arriba

(ah-ree-bah)

A hairy bar floating up in the air above everything.

down / below

abajo

(ah-bah-ho)

Someone smashing a *banjo down* into and *below* the ground.

turnaround

giro de vuelta

(gee-ro deh voo-el-tah)

The *gears* of a bike being turned around by a *vulture*.

entrance

entrada (f.)

(en-trah-dah)

An *adder entering* a building.
(Entering adder)

exit

salida (f.)

(sah-lee-dah)

A *salad leaving* a building.
(Leaving salad)

next to

cerca

(s-air-kah)

Someone standing *next to* a *circle* or *circus*.

in front
al frente
(al fren-teh)
A group of *all french fries* stood in front of an *elephant*.

behind
detrás
(deh-tr-ass)
A letter *D* standing *behind* an *ass*.

inside
dentro
(dent-roh)
A dentist rowing inside of your mouth.

outside
fuera de
(foo-air-ah deh)
Someone doing Kung-*Fu* moves in the *air outside*.

Conjunctions
Conjunciones

a
un (m.) / una (f.)
(oon / oo-nah)
Think Spanish for 1, uno. 'A' single thing.

the

el (m.) / la (f.)

(el / lah)

A band called *The El La* (The The The). With the name of the band written on the bass drum skin.

is

es

(ess)

A Spanish flag with 'is' written on it.

but

pero

(peh-roh)

Someone looking at pears and saying, "I like that *pear*
but not that *pear*.".

that

ese (m.) / esa (f.)

(ess-eh / ess-ah)

Looking at an *essay* someone has written and thinking
that is incredible!

this

esto (m.) / esta (f.)

(ess-toh / ess-tah)

A chef saying, *"This pesto pasta* is so nice."

or

O

(oh)

You need to pick an *oar* to go rowing with and you have to choose between two oars with giant *O*'s on the end.

(This oar *or* that oar)

to

a

(ah)

Is this the way *to* Amarillo?

(*Ah*-marillo)

and

y

(ee)

An 'E and Y' and another 'E and Y' and
another 'E and Y' all the way to infinity.
(A giant row of E's and Y's).

because

porque

(por-keh)

A *pork*chop floating around like a *bee* explaining 'because...'

for

para
(pah-rah)
A parrot saying para, para, para, para.
(*For* four times)

some

alguno (m.) / alguna (f.)

(al-goo-noh / al-goo-nah)

A big pile of *some goo*.

then

después

(des-poo-ess)

Showing someone a row of poos and saying, *"this poo is...then...* this poo is..."

like

similar

(see-mee-lar)

The word 'like' looking at itself in the mirror and *seeing* the word 'similar' as a reflection.

if

si

(see)

Looking out to *sea* to *see if* you can *see* the word *if* floating in it.

by

por

(pour)

Holding a jug *by* the handle and *pouring* it.

of
de
(deh)

A group *of D*'s acting like babies saying, *"deh-deh."*

Discover more at

www.draw-it-books.com

Follow

@drawitbooks

to stay up to date on all things **Draw It Books!**

Printed in Great Britain
by Amazon